The Fever Poems

poems by

KYLIE GELLATLY

Finishing Line Press
Georgetown, Kentucky

The Fever Poems

Copyright © 2021 by KYLIE GELLATLY
ISBN 978-1-64662-553-6 First Edition
All rights reserved under International and Pan-American Copyright Conventions. No part of this book may be reproduced in any manner whatsoever without written permission from the publisher, except in the case of brief quotations embodied in critical articles and reviews.

Publisher: Leah Huete de Maines
Editor: Christen Kincaid
Cover Art: Kylie Gellatly
Author Photo: Kylie Gellatly
Cover Design: Kylie Gellatly

Order online: www.finishinglinepress.com
also available on amazon.com

Author inquiries and mail orders:
Finishing Line Press
P. O. Box 1626
Georgetown, Kentucky 40324
U. S. A.

Table of Contents

Preface ix
a section through the catastrophe x

I

two years following to seek 1
I could stay here 2
let the clocks run down 3
a great many made many 4
there are a few names 5
the beckoning stops 6
look there and there 7
I shall fill in the deafness 8
the return of sunlight 9
the arc light 10
let me tell of the hearts 11
there was a hole 12
I will let you wait 13
night after night I communed 14
you followed me thus far 15
July with me 16

II

Miranda 21
our luck was not to last long 22
I fear I might have said goodbye 23
I know the end 24
fever night figures 25
land was useless 26
twenty years of my life 27
organs reach out from knives 28
I distinctly remember silver 29
dreaming would becoming restless 30
I assume you are looking down 31
it had been clear 32
an old metal hope 33
as the days offered to return 34

Miranda was to die 35

III

there is wind being slowly cut 39
four hundred feet high 40
I lift the floor 41
by the time the deal lost its lure 42
all I knew was fever 43
you know the storm went out 44
when I came across the heart 45
the ship 46

Acknowledgements

Preface

This is a body of found collage poetry sources from *The Arctic Diary of Russell Williams Porter* and constructed mostly over the course of one month in the summer of 2020. The work is a product of the isolation and anxiety of the first summer months during the pandemic and charts its way through the translation of that experience into found poetry. This process-based hybrid work, in its structured and confined space, lent itself to a depth of processing that allowed me to express a new voice—one that could adapt to the changes with an appetite and chew doom to a pulp, only to spit it out in a new form.

Williams' story was one of ambition, artistic vision, and survival in an unlivable climate and the words he wrote to describe the journey subjected themselves to an allegorical parallel once cut from his pages and rearranged onto mine. As these poems were written, the collection revealed itself to be a phantom, nearly gone, pleading for harmony and begging the attention of the reader to the finite lives we live.

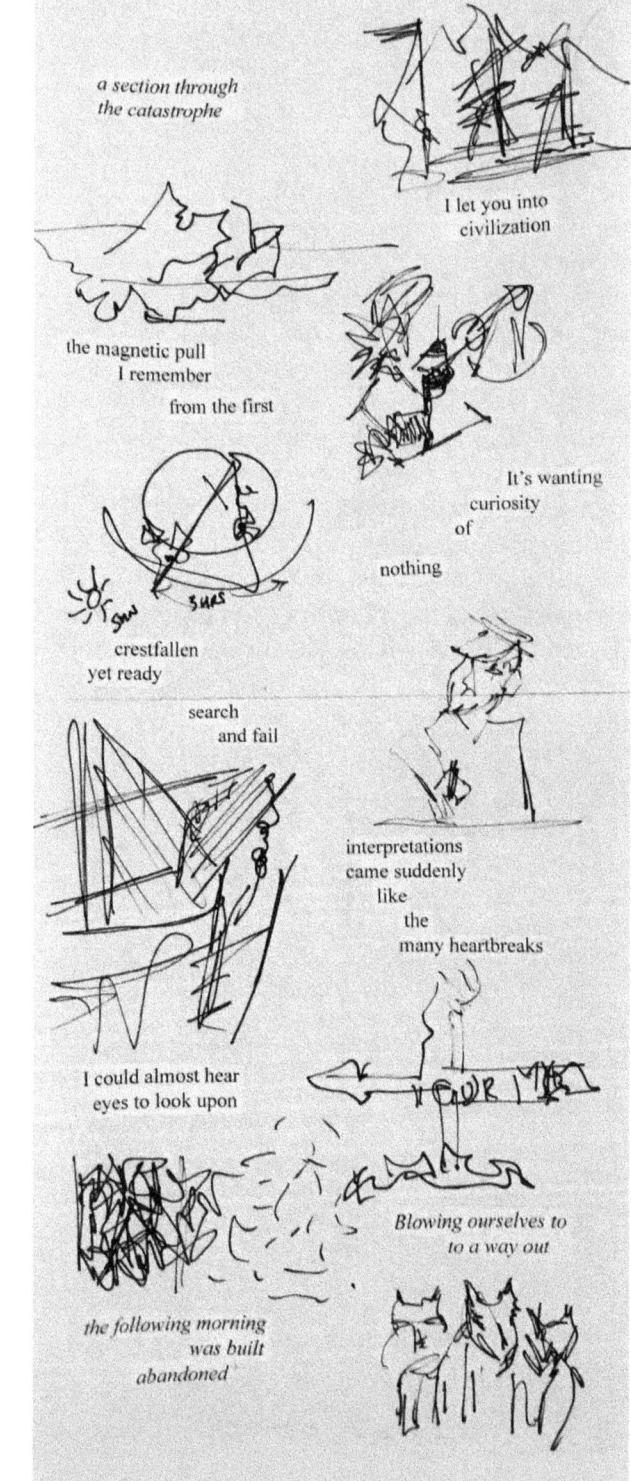

I.

Tropics and fevers

go hand in hand

year after year

none of them alike

two years following to seek

        two years
        following
        to seek
and at last
        we could see
        the range it was
                a horse's back
                      laid with grass and
                                streams for us
                                    to navigate
                                        so loaded was the water with
                            silk it rubbed against the night
                            we made contact with
                                            its grandeur and with
                                        this we made our way leaving

                to climb the thaw
to chance the wall the axe
          refused
                                    and we returned
                                    as though
                                      dependent on
                            several occasions
to
knife and sketch
                the wide field where
                        we were   bitten with the lure

                                        to follow the headwaters
                                              to persist

        we were at the drawing board   with the chance to begin

                      we were at the beginning
                    with the rewards of fever

I could stay here

                I could stay here
          shedding
            grass
               from my feet until
all landmarks disappear
        but there will be no
                      land

the scarred
        pinnacles will be the skin
of my lips as stiff as taut silk
      the stove of my body
    will be patient enough
      to dry a bed of roses
and I will be the spring
that crumbles away with time

      the gods will heave   down
                flatirons
        ground to pieces
and the fossilized jaws of vice
  will thrash
      through a once cliff
      handfuls of sand will
     make up my backbone
and my fingers will hold the earth
     like worms craving death

          but no—instead
    I will replace the legs
that give way to high winds

and I will wait for the meteorite

let the clocks run down

let the clocks run down and subside in the ether
           it is at home in steep walls not daring to be
                      released to me

                                let us pause for a moment and strike balance

                  while the fog forges each minute into fever
                              graves beckon to burn
                                    and shape time

                          but I am not   the seeker
                                for longitude is nothing but
                          the difference between time and
              the observer

                        the purpose of
                        clocks is out of my life each year

                                        again
                                I drop into the
                                    life span well along

          I might have arrived in architecture

it came with a letter
        "I will land you
                and
            doubt
    the spring of the year"

                I would live over again
                        merged with the tongue in need of tuning
                            choked with the monsters of parentheses

            but even
                  sound is an unbroken expanse
                        among
                        the greater taking—
              of time and fever and nothing more

a great many made many

a great many
                made many with an ax
             decisioned or approved
                  the good
                      in either case
       the mind
            obtained to stand
                        the summer
      the night being clear
      the last desires I had said
              I loved so well

                    I ran
denied having reached the summit
it was only a rock from the grave
that this boulder had taken for its new
                      polished face

  Later I found the headstone
       granite bound   so that I might swing
the pendulum for the last time and ring
the heavy instrument of brass and cast iron
        that I was awakened by
     so I could hear the names

    across the boulder   recognition would shortly appear

there are a few names

    there are a few names
  for which no verification can be obtained
                        the goddess the house the guard the trigger
                        the doctor the earth the infant the year
                        the stomach the anxiety

      a normal agony
   blowing up
the brittle a gale in all hands
the baby peeking out from her red ribbon

                                      I remember dropping
                           to yell and dance with no protection
                                        never to leave
                           the hammer moved in
                                  the oil written then
                         to no avail knowing the gun
                       was my belly round and wheeled

                  the bullet
              she bit at the wound
                is what ailed
      if it was red you could take it for granted
                            and if it was alabaster
              though coal-laden
              the wreckage
                      was picked up

   the gun was a mother busy with her summer litter
 nevertheless bringing us home with her heavy salvage

                    young vessels should be at the grindstone
                          trying to reason with
                                  the stronger
                  to swing their own pendulums

the beckoning stops

        the beckoning stops in the quarry

  —all disappear   gold so grave that
                       sorrow follows
                         its treacherous surface

  the return of the sun has aroused a feeling
    akin to birdskin badly bitten

water vulnerable   held up to the light

    that elusive siren—
hadn't she left us any balance?

          what was mica before   is now
                             the only star

I think of it as nothing
    but the desired effect   of life's admitted value

      but don't ever forget
    that gravel is thrown   at night

look there and there

       look there and there and there
those floating specks are hundreds of baled papers
          bent up like two bears dancing
dear woman your retina must abandon the sun and you must
         remove the matches from my hand
             we will then hear the mirror grieve its light

               now that we have held morning like a dead dog
    your words resound as vivid
                    as a deep sea wooing in low tones—
         for me to drop my net into
     and walk across with shaking hands

I shall fill in the deafness

I shall fill in the deafness
   of the women who told you
     to be good
with a seasoned conviction that hell
  is damp wood in a virgin's heart
    and that gold will always
      be a chased animal with skin
  torn to pieces

I was sore at heart
        a lavender tint my head
      like tinder
hair-raised and stranded
I tried to shout in the wilds
   of the dining room when dynamite
     was handled without word

but it did not end
   the resounding hammering
     at the fire that your obsession
       brought you

the return of sunlight

the return of sunlight
that we molded
with lamped hands
carries along
a warm wind
the craved fruit of effort
        gorged by relief
like bread
on the table
before my son
        these pleasant suns
of monotony
do you see
how magnetically
they rise
how the ascent
follows as steady
as a line of flags
our faces
day and night
overflowing with
the long lines of
the new year

the arc light

the arc light went out
and several vague forms emerged
in the dark living room
they spoke to me in women's notes

"we are not hunters
our knives are but mirrors and shovels
they shine so we can dig ourselves
out of darkness"

but I myself have no food without killing
and when my erratic days are through
I will lie on the green floor
with the midnight sun—not under

one woman slid her knife beneath a thin layer
of my flesh—"gold gold gold!"
but at times the gold is only a mirror
faintly iridescent—a window full of moonlight

the strange contrast between death and dawn
is an intimation of night's secret council
here to let me choose a knife or a tomb
for the skin of the magnetic morning

let me tell of the hearts

let me tell of the hearts lying
in a seam a hundred feet long
like mica in a gold mine
beating under the simple plane
of persistence
I had added fever to fever
I dared time with a knife blade
I did not believe it was my own
I was asleep and floating on a letter
I lay a captive in chains
I stormed the ramparts
I dashed to the very spur
I bided my time and the coup de grace
I had nothing to do with the shipwreck
I would bring back the news
and my respects
     as usual a crate of oranges
and an indentation in my knife-holding hand
my sole regret a passion for the bitter pill
mining indicated the demon of mine
was referring to the heart
the little-known interior
already forming in my mind
going along full speed being drawn down
and introduced to tear down
almost every trick
there would be something for the heartbreak
the miles of ice and the years of dense fog
anything to stimulate the heart
with this profound deduction
the penned line
is blank as to just what happened
but the diary indicates I knew
that this man turned doors there
and unlocked its secret

there was a hole

                              there was a hole leading down
                                    my first thought
                                              but when I slid
                              in the flickering light of a bed in salt
                                         I could have seen
                                                days drift by
                                          will you go with me?
                                             I would
                  the severed
                     red light that held us to the doom
                          slowly moved away in the darkness

                                      we subsisted on salt and rocks

                                                  I feared
                                             for nearly a week
                      there still remained room in sigh
                              to circle round and round over head

                                  out we ran on
                              bad weather and
                                  intended to drive in search of succor

we were found lying beside the water and
                                                carried away

we have many an island but we hope for one hundred

I will let you wait

I will let you
       wait for
           the effect
following
     you up
         to take
hands and knees if necessary
to give the
       fever
inoculated with the virus of
vicissitudes

when it finally arrived
  I had become
  small
in person
my decision
          seemed to beg
this journey
back and
      I am sure
I must choose
the great
reflection
and thus
the harrowing details

but I must not consider it
  the only right thing
  for summer
       in shipwreck

night after night I communed

       night after night I communed with
                         time as I
began to realize the significance of just what
this very face built

        and at last the secret came out—light
   for you taught me how to labor in love

            whatever
          brought out
             the spirits played across the rocky
                     interior and into our hands

                    so our backs became a valley
              from wall to wall almost continuous
                and our footing an archipelago
                            with its smoking volcanoes
                    feeling for wood
                    to build fever

                  for we know
             a big fire will let us forget
                      the dim in the distance
       and remember that love
          was not light
     before it reached your eye

you followed me thus far

you followed me thus far in my first flirtation with such gravity
                  that icy goddess who had treated me so
          with only the clothes on my back
              I found
            that I had decided
     the reaction was quite the opposite

       far back in
            the door
haunting melodies of the dancing
   floor the nights without darkness—all served
                a stronger determination to go farther

                 would you like to go along and
                              welcome another year?
                         would I? we did

                 I had learned
               all I had imagined
                       we even discovered that I lived my own love
                                 which finally took shape

        we lived time together
          in the skin boats
               of accretion

     returning to the
        curious
              who would justly conclude that
                   my lesson had made the pledge

we were to be one
      of a couple in the corner of a
trail that walk through
           the interior of the rest of the mornings

July with me

July with me
my sunny jumble of peaks
my dear pack animal
my sweet box canyon
the last of the last
of the stone-flagged flings
a week is but
a year after year
with islands
of haystacks
that I can hear from here
it is the opposite of

                    November
                that is fit for
                      changes
          all souls pulse now
         when a form holds
                aloft a glass
              or is it a crow
            the pledge made
                into paper
                  weathered
                in our hands
            all things come
say it again—now wait

July with me
my sunny jumble of peaks
my dear pack animal
my sweet box canyon
the last of the last
of the stone-flagged flings
a week is But
a Year after year
With islands
of haystacks
that I can hear from here
it is the opposite of

November
that is fit for
changes
All souls pulse now
when A form holds
aloft a glass
or is it a crow
the pledge made
into paper
weathered
in our hands
All things come
Say it again—now wait

II.

what was coming
was not
those fugitive glimpses of the
island,
barely opened before it was closed

Miranda

I had eighteen crossings to the side of the stricken, Miranda.

When we lay on the stern and asked for time to confer,

creating the others who now know that letter.

At the time, Miranda, a slight uneasiness was coming.

Around midnight, a red light arrived. Broken, he was gone, Miranda.

Miranda, for us to stand by, seemed comparable to few words.

Such was their verdict, Miranda, to bless our relief.

I have since been told that this fall was born in physics, Miranda.

Beginning to give way, under their revelry in broad daylight—

I remained busy, Miranda, kept rather careful observations.

Miranda, I must have been dreaming. Yes I was dreaming,

because the dancing and the nights saved us enough,

and back we went, Miranda.

our luck was not to last long

our luck was not to last long housing on
                                                mountains
it was remarkably quiet considering but it was true
            the moonlight
     forced high in the air as
                     the engine waited for the final
                                dash each one of us
                        returned to stand on the black water
        hoping to be in that last wail of the
                violins midnight
                     announced beautifully
all this framed the oily floor
  and the half-wild music of
        an unforgettable commotion above

there is a
      mute room half-filled
with time now to remove anything of value nothing
                                          was gone
                equal to a hive of idle hours no present
                            sunk there only dusk
        the long night left no trace

I fear I might have said goodbye

   I fear
         I might have said
                 goodbye
            I'm done
not the words I used but the
               way out of
                      there would have been
something like a mocking

                   a candid expression of their feelings
                       was somewhere
                          to intercept it found and induced
                             to try it alone

                         the long
                             covered
                                     siren looked up to face
                    home thick fog
                    looked awfully
                             massive over the horizon remained still
               to build
               to assist
               to accompany us home
                             like an iron vessel with great ceremony

I know the end

I know the end of the world
    is never forced to wait
but arrives between
  false alarms
    while veeing birds
  are dragged
      over raised eyes

    I never got a word in living
  below the horizon lingering
      over houses breathing
     it is true
      that nothing is
     as wanted as
    open water

         I stay only
    to burn what's left
  of the inferior coal
  mined from everything
that has yet
  to be heard

fever night figures

fever
   night
       figures
       point
       where
          one step away
   there
       is a contradiction

                 but
                    fever
             kept on calling
        to an invisible   evening
              to a person standing   beckoning
              to a portal
              to a paradox
            to   a variation
              all its own

              to know what's
unknown
to satisfy me

            only to return
       too often

land was useless

                                               land
                              was useless along
                                      distances scarred and tasted

        we started to back out as though bound
                                  we yelled from ashore

     the climax
poorly charted you scrimmaged
                                    the sensation across a paragraph

           what
    you're taking is the forgotten towering
        fever that brooked the only
                           wind

       what I think
     at times of great
transpiring: is if you cornered them
                   you would hear
                    the whole
                         was
                            the vessel
                  but you think you're the
                    short cut

            once
         having a
      taste
upon the tongue that I was never able to name
   I ran a mad dash
      for water
         for the first time thoroughly
            tasted
       what seemed fatal to me
                                  and once
                                    quite definite

twenty years of my life

                twenty years of my life
                   the pictures
                      waste
there is only one direction—yes
                          over the striking moon
                   and the striking recollection
                        being torn out
                          to swing out
                 when the audience of the clear sky
              seems suddenly to be
                     old abandoned
                          rotting ice

                                millenniums telling
                           the known announcing
                              "you're alive"
                  hundreds who well know stayed only
                        out of a submerged appreciation
                  for loss
                          failures intrigued them—

           we must be
              kind there is no oil

                        I refer to
                    the historian of
                the living: "we
                    might
                keep all hands"

      but the storm that holds us in sight
            blows away the day and
we are furiously burning with
thirst

organs reach out from knives

organs reach out from knives
      and valuable days go missing
        what was carved out
           would have been hope

  precious time was discovered at the fingers
    and uncanny knowledge
      at the head

          the
      crowd is a miracle
        twenty miles it
     spoons
    out of wood

not knowing just what would show up in the year
    we soon pick
      some hundred on the qui vive
       heavy
       with
      the rise and fall
        of consequence
     dragged considerable distances over
       affairs to move
   down runways of staves

         now at higher edges
         we make
           rocks into handles
       while the murderous
         serve
        rather than go back
       to the running
        side of sound

  it will not be long before a word is overheard

I distinctly remember silver knives

      I distinctly remember
                silver knives
                         on the breath
          glimpses of the night
            were at last
          passing this imaginary line
          we were nearing the
doubt
    dividing
islands into salt

        dead
   pause the hush it did
 go on
and on making
  pressure
to take on
skins and salts
 to
generate a slight current of
                  these
            strong mouths
some desire
  too often not to crawl along
       the memory and return
              time to time
                    to let this hold fall
  I see you
    loose with me
      and a-snare
 promises have proved a delusion
  expressed
into open water
  the loom of
       our position
welcomes
     the best of
  the last
to tell us more
we never had the luck
          we were told
                had dispatched
                in our souls

dreaming would become restless

dreaming
        would become restless
           after the   fever
                 primarily because of
     a fascination for the stars
        while living
with a two-inch mirror

        I scarcely knew what struck
   'til I had gone
     and begged reverse

perfection needed
            this new challenge
                      and taught
        that nothing would
     come   willingly

  within ten degrees of
    insidious disease
      I said
     stop me
  and remained
    for a short time
   with the ill-fated
              design

I assume you are looking down

I assume you are looking
 down on the sun directly

      just what are you thinking of?
         whether we are
            gaining or losing?

              it is the only means
        time expresses by degrees

                    there is a wind
              through the vertical circle
                I hold vigil with the
                      light moving
                over the crosshairs

          hoping to be thrown together again

      the events are
figments of my imagination and I
    numb
        myself

                it is not much of a reward
      to be the only piece of new land
            smoking come morning

it had been clear

it had been clear
                I was to run
   like the alcohol that went
   through my fingers

                          to the usual
                  vantage points
           within
      sight of the sun
to quench the days
                    without silver linings

   I could
          use the dogs   to tie up the
   horizon now
      rid of elms

      and I would see
   from the glacial
     pressure ridges
              that fever was
                        to return

an old metal hope

                    an old
                            metal hope stalled me
when the flies and mosquitoes solemnly
                                    retired speaking

              I received a rambling
                      museum
  to bring back some
father
    and started pointing
        to the
  unmapped swamps and
                    remnants of
  standing pianos

                  I saw for the first time
that the yellow bark of a tree
   was a terse remark
      for when we lost one
           beginning
            after another

        so I combed the mountains
                      for a horse
that could barely be seen high up in the trees

I wanted to know why
she climbed so high

        and to hide what I collected
to pack it away in her diamond hitch

as the days offered to return

as the days
        offered to return
      the time they killed
   fewer mouths seemed
          to meet him

                her admiration still not gone
         unlike the
    drift storms
       that forced the heavens
            out of the way

                 his frozen
                    heel was replaced
          with light loads
        of destination
     knowing that nothing
descended to an earth shifting

      while several balloons
were made to reach her he
     stretched unbroken

         as she used up her
        gravity
   securing too heroic a horizon

Miranda was to die

        Miranda was to die of heart failure
      while ascending from a depth known
but seeing that the faults didn't take she said
          "I would not recognize you void
              wait for me until I do"

        when night overtook she wrote
          a memory of former love
   on a sheet in salt—an inscription
    long past and in pieces bent split
she then saw what fleeted and tried to reach
behind the viscous dark of her watercolor blood

  the name of fever sounded and sank below
within a few feet of truth wading in the ice water
  the seeds of unrest had at last ceased calling
   never again knocking at her through the air

    Miranda was a tear in the side of absence
with her deviled spaces almost halfway to the moon
no horses barred with her nothing restless or firing

    the last we saw of her she was undisturbed
     deriving knowledge from all other evenings
      she who waited abreast the temperature
        of such a strange and cold steam
          for the rest of her memory

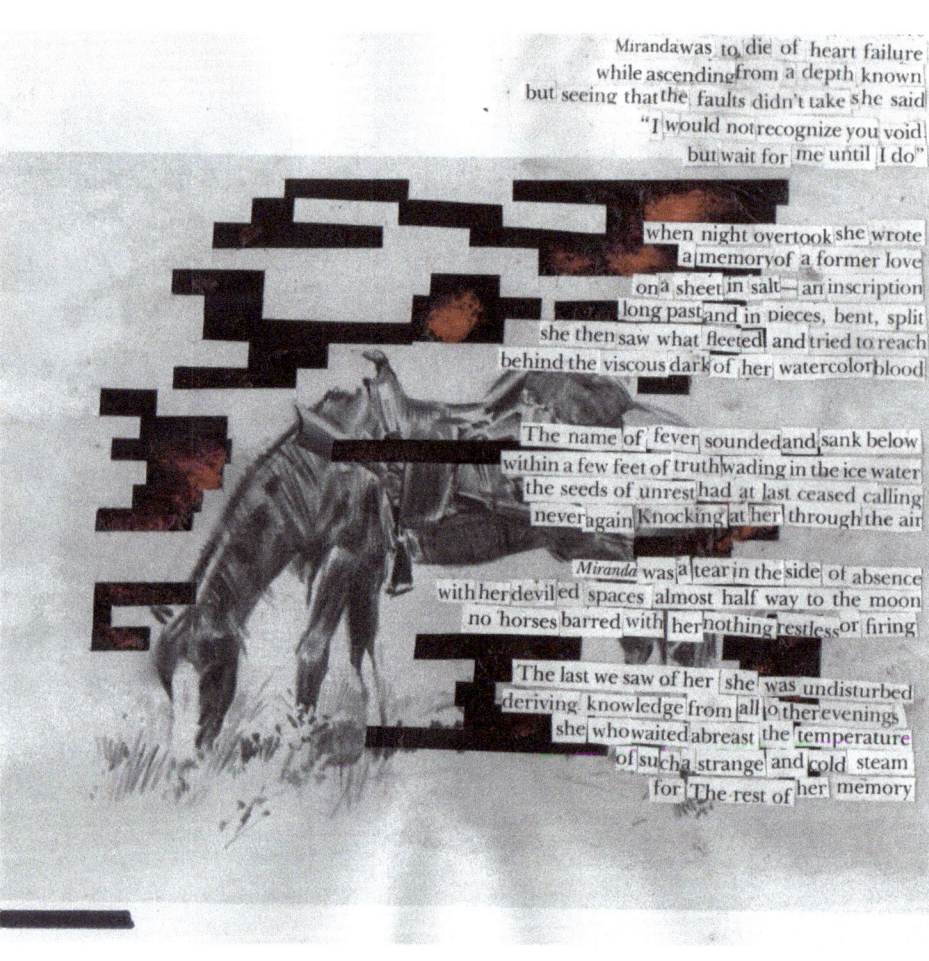

Miranda was to die of heart failure
while ascending from a depth known
but seeing that the faults didn't take she said
"I would not recognize you void
but wait for me until I do"

when night overtook she wrote
a memory of a former love
on a sheet in salt— an inscription
long past and in pieces, bent, split
she then saw what fleeted and tried to reach
behind the viscous dark of her watercolor blood

The name of fever sounded and sank below
within a few feet of truth wading in the ice water
the seeds of unrest had at last ceased calling
never again Knocking at her through the air

Miranda was a tear in the side of absence
with her deviled spaces almost half way to the moon
no horses barred with her nothing restless or firing

The last we saw of her she was undisturbed
deriving knowledge from all of the evenings
she who waited abreast the temperature
of such a strange and cold steam
for The rest of her memory

III.

                                  An hour
             without
                                        catastrophe

                as vivid as
                                  falling into
ice water
             drawn
                       with
                                      fever

there is wind being slowly cut

        there is wind being slowly cut
    like glass when I open my eyes
            to the errors of
                      delicate sense

            I use my
            third name
                when breaking
        the long knife

    but I grow fainter and fainter
measuring frozen tides and writing with my jaw

        the angel
        lavish with choice
                dares to strike through my heart

        she is shrouded
like an invasive surgeon
            with her worrying axe

            the fool's divine spark
       forever coming loose
from my cup as it falls from my crossing fingers

four hundred feet high

four
       hundred feet high
              I leaned over
                    the raucous cries none of us
                         caught the eye near high noon
                                down
                                     miles through
                              the fall
                              soon to lie in the lap of plenty

              it was
     where it was for it undoubtedly burrowed
the houses of the gold seekers in sand
        it was night that
        crushed the rocks

                    we never revisited the spot
                        I have no knowledge of
                  the extreme end of the crater
                                union of
                                      man taken
                            to be a trench
                              that might have been a cannon ball
         when fossils essayed to go on with the decision to abandon land

I lift the floor

I lift   the
    floor in one corner concentrating on
                          virgin land
         no sign of it anywhere
        only footprints of the
            feast
    after which I was wise about
          the taste of oil
wiser about the taste of blood

       I
    am
  unbearable and
unwilling to give up the ghost
   for its worth in scrap
  I tell you I chopped off the head
like a roof the storms had blown
        regretting that
         the best
           was over too soon

by the time the deal lost its lure

by the time the deal
        lost its lure and
                settled
                      an examination showed
                              the manuscript of
            small rocks a mile away
            silhouetted
    and open   bound
                      somehow

            with
              the
       pyramid point of
              speed we dashed into
           morning
                      to go home
              for a summer
       soon pounding

the sight of our first
                great disappointment
                  pulled away
                    broken
              against the sky
          as old and young
                  as the
           engine

all I knew was fever

        all I knew was
        fever
        after a month
        of no resistance
        after I could see
        beyond the ranges

        I know what it is

           somehow
           my own
           beckoning
           ceased
           to lure

        I remember
        clear as day
        a bribe of
           obvious folly
           many thrills
anything of a descriptive nature
           returning

        it is doubt raised dire
        a voyage
           describes
        retreat
        for human embrace
        be thankful
        to see
        the temptation
the crushing defeats few favors

        this domain of mine
        surrounding
        the indefinable lure
        and the
        silence of many
        saying go
before I had had enough

you know the storm went out

                                                            you know the
                                                                  storm
                                                                went out and
                  I believed you were down there
                              for it has never
                                        been
              a different story
           living as a key
forged   full
           of hell

  a severe shock
reached
  forward
three days we
feared you had gone
        I was worried
        you
    were held
               with it
                    and
              sketched
       memory
in the fog

   everybody
          speaks of this
recollection
   in
    a meridian headed for
   farewell
       twenty years
was about as much good as
                         circling
         a black eye

to have made you this trouble it's been nothing

when I came across the heart

when I came across
 the heart of this little hunt
dented open
 by starvation fish

 I ran this knife
to measure the flow of
 melt and in tasteless time
 I filled two cups

the heat was a hunger
 so great it left
 their bodies

 only to be forced
carving out
 the rigors of a
 heart now bone

 out of the water
 you must warp
 and to go home you
 must point

but it is in this
 way that we
 island ourselves

the ship

the ship was the rib of reason

the ship was unable to follow me

the ship was frowning with a fist in her face

the ship was a very quiet widowhood

the ship was nothing but a long-hand manuscript

the ship was negatives converted to positives

the ship was now experienced in looking

the ship was an off-year stripped bare

the ship was a council of war decreed

the ship was the guttural ejaculations of fear

the ship never happened but could not be denied

the ship was limping back to swell up

the ship was beginning to be an alarm

the ship was right there on the floor
        while this book was written

the ship was the rib of reason

the ship was unable to follow me

the ship was frowning with a fist in her face

the ship was a very quiet widowhood

the ship was nothing but a long-hand manuscript

the ship was negatives converted to positive

the ship was now experienced in looking

the ship was an off year Stripped bare

the ship was a council of war decreed

the ship was the guttural ejaculations of fear

the ship never happened But could not be denied

the ship was limping back to swell up

the ship was beginning to be an alarm

the ship was right there on the floor
while this book was written

ACKNOWLEDGMENTS

To the editors who gave homes to these poems in their original visual forms and for their amazing work and championship of visual poetry—Jennifer Pilch, Sarah Feng, Jacob Rivers, Shari Altman & Rebecca Siegel, Bianca & Walter Stone, Beth Gordon, Jen Karetnick, Seth Copeland, Whitney Kerutis, Joshua Roark—thank you for providing space for these poems and for your championship of visual poetry:

> *COUNTERCLOCK*—"the beckoning stops", "look there and there", "I know the end", "a great many made many", "twenty years of my life"
> *Feral*—"there is wind being slowly cut", "as the days offered to return", "four hundred feet high", "night after night", "the return of sunlight"
> *GASHER*—"I could stay here", "I lift the floor", "I distinctly remember silver", "you know the storm went out", "there are a few names", "organs reach out"
> *Iterant Magazine*—"I shall fill in the deafness", "Miranda was to die", "two years following", "the ship"
> *La Vague Journal*—"an old metal hope"
> *Literary North*—"when I came across the heart"
> *Malasaña Magazine*—"dreaming would become restless", "all I knew was fever", "a section through the catastrophe"
> *Palette Poetry*—"land was useless"
> *Petrichor*—"July with me"
> *Roads Taken: An Anthology of Contemporary Vermont Poetry* (Green Writers Press)—"the arc light", "our luck was not to last long"
> *SWWIM*—"the arc light"

My gratitudes to Christen Kincaid and those at Finishing Line Press who have promoted this work into the hands of so many and helped to share a vision. Thank you to the Vermont Studio Center for the time, space, and encouragement you have provided me over the years, and to Liz Powell, Jensen Beach, and Darcie Abbene of the Creative Writing Department at Northern Vermont University for the many opportunities to do so. A special thank you to Kirsten Miles and the team at Tupelo Press for encouraging these poems through their 30/30 Project and for making sure they came to light during such dark times; additional thanks to all of the donors who helped support such a heated month of poetry. To Sarah Audsley and Daniel Zeese, for being there while this book was written and for sharing a bubble in the early days of the pandemic. To Melanie Risch, for your instrumental articulation of the relationship between book and body and for the inspiration to cut up books. Thank you to Django Koenig for the gift of *The Arctic Diary of Russel Williams Porter*.

To Erin Adair-Hodges, Taneum Bambrick, Ilya Kaminsky, Jenny Molberg, and Bianca

Stone—I am so grateful for the time and care you took with these poems and for offering so much in your poetry, teaching, and openness. Warm thanks for the support, emotional and otherwise, to the following at Mount Holyoke College: Andrea Lawlor, Jasmine Errico, Peiyun Jiang, Alejandra Cabezas, Flannery Langton, Liz Lewis, and Olivia Brandwine.

Lastly, I disclose a multitude of thanks to my family for their never-ending celebration and for teaching me the values of voice and persistence; to the friends and mentors that have listened to me, and the many many poets who keep me going; and to Eamon—for being so present and supportive throughout this journey with me and for always having a favorite line.

Kylie Gellatly's poetry has appeared in *Action Spectacle, Counterclock, DIAGRAM, Feral, Gasher, Iterant Magazine, La Vague Journal, Literary North, Malasana Magazine, Palette Poetry, Petrichor, Ruminate,* and *SWWIM*. Kylie is Editor-in-Chief of *Mount Holyoke Review*, Book Reviews Editor for *Green Mountains Review*, and a poetry reader for *Pleiades*. She has been awarded the Factory Hollow Press Scholarship to the Juniper Writing Institute, was shortlisted for the 2020 Disquiet Prize, and has received two fellowships to the Vermont Studio Center. Kylie lives in Western Massachusetts and is a Frances Perkins Scholar at Mount Holyoke College. For more, visit www.kyliegellatly.com

www.ingramcontent.com/pod-product-compliance
Lightning Source LLC
Chambersburg PA
CBHW042145160426
43201CB00022B/2412